VIEWPOINTS
of a
COMMODITY
TRADER

By
ROY LONGSTREET

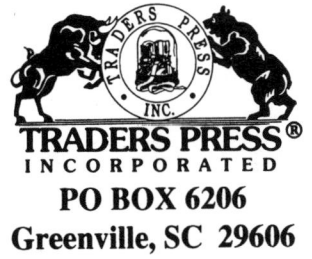

TRADERS PRESS®
INCORPORATED
PO BOX 6206
Greenville, SC 29606

*Books and Gifts
for Investors and Traders*

Copyright© 1967 by Roy W. Longstreet. All rights reserved. Printed in the United States of America. No part of this publication may be reproduced, stored in a retrieval system, or transmitted, in any form or by any means, electronic, mechanical, photocopying, recording, or otherwise, without the prior written permission of the publisher.

Reprinted by agreement with Lifetime Books, Inc., February 1997

Publications of Traders Press, Inc.:

Commodity Spreads: A Historical Chart Perspective (Dobson)
The Trading Rule That Can Make You Rich* (Dobson)
A Complete Guide to Trading Profits (Paris)
The Professional Commodity Trader (Kroll)
Jesse Livermore: Speculator King (Sarnoff)
Understanding Fibonacci Numbers (Dobson)
Winning Market Systems (Appel)
How to Trade in Stocks (Livermore)
Commodity Spreads (Smith)
Day Trading with Short Term Price Patterns (Crabel)
Understanding Bollinger Bands (Dobson)
Chart Reading for Professional Traders (Jenkins)
Geometry of Stock Market Profits (Jenkins)

Please contact Traders Press to receive our current catalog describing these and many other books and gifts of interest to investors and traders.

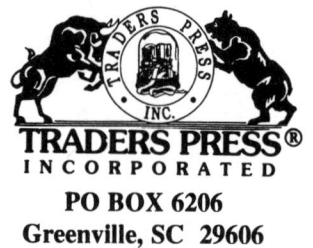

TRADERS PRESS®
INCORPORATED
**PO BOX 6206
Greenville, SC 29606**

*Books and Gifts
for Investors and Traders*

*800-927-8222 Fax 864-298-0221 864-298-0222 Tradersprs@aol.com
http://Traderspress.com*

To the memory of Coach Howard Wood who taught that the only way is the hard way

Illustrations by Martha Z. Ohlemeyer

VIEWPOINTS OF A COMMODITY TRADER

INTRODUCTION

Many traders feel that the key to successful and profitable trading lies solely in finding the "perfect system," or at least a highly profitable trading method. They fail to realize, and never learn, that without understanding **themselves**, and mastering the psychological aspect of trading, they will never be truly successful. Without the proper discipline and dedication, any system or method becomes ineffective. In this classic book, the attitude, mental discipline, and philosophy required to become a successful trader are explored by veteran trader Roy Longstreet.

TRADERS PRESS distributes hundreds of books, courses, and gifts of interest to traders and investors and periodically publishes a traders catalog which describes these items. A free copy is available by contacting **Traders Press, Inc.**, PO Box 6206, Greenville, SC 29606; 800-927-8222; Fax 864-298-0221; Tradersprs@aol.com; http://traderspress.com.

Edward D. Dobson
Greenville, SC
February, 1997

Foreword

THIS BOOK has been written because my contacts with individuals who trade in commodities, or more particularly who *try* to trade in commodities, convince me that it is needed; and because it is difficult to watch people suffer repeatedly from making basic errors and then watch others follow in their footsteps. And yet advice is too often misunderstood when given in person.

I am sure that much of what I write will seem trite, commonplace, and of little value to some. I am also sure that much of what I write will be worth repeating time and time again because, human nature being what it is, very few traders do the right thing at the right time. They know, like St. Paul, that what they are doing is not always what they should be doing.

Like any man's store of wisdom, what I have set down has been acquired over a lifetime of reading, listening to others, and just living. It is my intention to pass these ideas on to others to help them learn from experience. With the passage of time, it is no longer possible for me to remember where every idea contained in these pages came from. It is not my intention to fail to give due credit where it is due.

Roy W. Longstreet

A Good Man

To Know

"KNOW THYSELF," Socrates said a long time ago and it's still good advice.

Most of the traders who lose money in commodities do so primarily because they don't know what they want to do.

I've heard it said that unhappiness consists of not knowing what you want and killing yourself to get it. This is certainly true in commodity trading, and it's a situation which must not be allowed to continue.

Until you ask yourself and get honest answers to such questions as: Who am I? What do I want to get from commodity trading? How can I best use my talent and my power (money) to get what I want?—until you do this, there are few, if any, advisory services or brokers who can be of much help to you.

It is important that you do not fool yourself. Don't even try. You just might do it. It is not easy to make

Viewpoints of a Commodity Trader

money, particularly a lot of money, in commodity trading. But you can do it—if you will pay the price. The price, simply stated, is enlightened self-discipline. You must have a program. You must know your program. You must follow your program.

Making Money With Money

"I HAVE MADE MONEY from no money. I have lost money with money, and I have made back the money I lost. Now I must learn to make money with money." This statement, made by a successful trader whom I visited in Rotterdam in the summer of 1963, has stimulated thought.

My observations lead to the conclusion that it is a very real problem. History is replete with instances that it is more difficult to make money with money than to make money without money; this seems particularly true in commodity trading. There is an adage that has come down through the ages that says: "A speculator cannot die rich. If he does, he dies before his time."

The problem seems to be of two parts: the character of the market; the ability and ambition of the individual.

Can one who has money continue to do as he did before he had money and be successful? The answer would seem to be No. The structure of the market is such that it is possible for one to start with very little and build a small fortune without much knowledge or information or understanding. With-the-market trading will do it. The difficulty comes when one's position becomes so large that it is watched by other traders. Now he must have knowledge. A little learning becomes dangerous. He can no longer go with the trend in all of his positions. His knowledge must be adequate to permit him to take positions against the market. Since it is never possible to know everything about anything, he is in constant danger. No longer is he dealing with small profits and small losses. One who has mastered the art of small profits and small losses may have difficulty in adjusting to a program of huge profits and huge losses. The stress points are different.

Perhaps the most important part of the problem is the trader who has come suddenly to a position of importance. Sudden success is heady medicine. Few people can adjust to it quickly. He generally feels that he knows more than he really does.

Successful trading requires four things: knowledge, disciplined courage, money, and the energy to merge the first three properly. Far too many traders try to substitute money for brains and courage, ignoring the principle that a fool and his money are soon parted.

Your First Loss

EXPECT AND ACCEPT. These words apply particularly to the practice of taking losses. Everyone who trades in commodities must at some time take a loss. Those who *expect* to do so and *accept* this fact gracefully will be successful in trading. Those who do not expect to do so will prejudice their judgment and allow emotions rather than reason to guide them.

Anyone who trades in commodities takes the position that he knows something that the market has not discounted, or he is taking the position that something will occur in the future that will cause a price change. In either case, there is some chance of being wrong.

Under such circumstances the problem is to know as quickly as possible when you are in error and then to take action to cut your losses to the minimum—hence, the saying, "Your first loss is your smallest loss."

I urge you to be on the lookout for signs that you

are wrong. Then admit it and run quickly from your position and accept your loss gracefully. Control any emotional desire to blame yourself or someone else. Above all, guard against any infantile reactions when you lose. Reconsider your reasons and judgment that led to your decision to take the position. Often the fault will lie in part or entirely with information you used and not your judgment. And remember the market itself can make a mistake. This state of mind will permit you to take advantage of the next opportunity. Those who brood over their losses always miss the next opportunity, which more than likely will be profitable.

Trading Is an Art

Is IT POSSIBLE to make money with money in commodity trading? Is it possible to do so on a grand scale —not a million dollars, but many, many millions? Can there be a General Motors in commodity trading?

The answer is clearly, Yes. The big question is, How?

The great philosopher Emerson gave the answer many years ago when he stated that a man is as a tree and his wealth is as a vine. The vine can grow no higher than the tree.

The evidence is conclusive that commodity trading is an art. To be successful at it one must be an artist. Such a trader can scale the heights of accomplishment, realizing achievements comparable to those of a renowned concert pianist, or a painter whose works merit a place in the great galleries of the world.

What, then, are the attributes needed by one who

would be a true artist in the world of commodities? There are many. A few are vital. Such men will be wise, be mighty, be already rich.

He who is wise learns from every man. He who is mighty has achieved control over his most formidable adversary, himself. He who is rich is satisfied with his lot. "He who seeks silver only will never be satisfied with silver."

There remains one other essential ingredient to making money with money and keeping it. It will require organized effort. One individual, acting as an individual, cannot do it. Time and energy are vital forces.

It is not easy to succeed in this great adventure. But it is not impossible. Success, when it comes, will be so sweet because it is so difficult.

New Goals

It was an entry in a very old diary. I have always liked the idea it expressed. Perhaps you will too.

The entry was from the journal of Thomas Cooper, a millwright from Ohio and a member of one of the overland wagon trains to California after the gold strike of 1848. It reads, in part, as follows:

"Our goal at last! Truly, this journey has been long and hard. Tonight, within the circle of the train, there is much gladness and merriment. But there is a kind of sadness too, which many have expressed and which I feel also—that our long journey, however difficult, is coming to its end.

"We will miss the real satisfaction we felt, as individuals and as a group banded together, as we met squarely and surmounted the obstacles of the trail and the obstacles which each of us had built in our own minds. I think we will all miss those early mornings on the trail, as we wondered what the new day would bring. I know that I will. . . ."

The passage of 120 years has not changed the truth of what this pioneer was saying. The most glorious moments of life are not the days of success but those days when you feel rise in you a challenge to life and the promise of future accomplishment.

It was my privilege for many years to work with and for William H. Danforth, founder of Ralston Purina Company. He knew and taught a good lesson —to complete a goal once set and then immediately set a new goal. He knew what I consider to be one of the major truths of life—that we must always have new goals before us. We are at our best and we are happiest when we are striving mightily to attain them.

We never stand still. The world does not and we cannot. Unless we progress, we go backwards. Change brings opportunity.

We are setting new goals just a notch higher than the old ones in the knowledge that step by step we build our fortune and our wisdom. Each success is built on a previous success.

Strength

PERHAPS ONE OF THE GREAT MISTAKES made by all of us in trading commodities is to force ourselves to make judgments when tired. Our market judgments should be good judgments. To be so, they should spring spontaneously from a clear, untroubled mind in a strong body. The Greeks, who were among the first of civilized people to promote good logic and freedom of thinking, realized this when they started the Olympics.

How many times have we been astounded by the success associated with raw, brutal force? Persistent, unremitting effort directed toward a worthy goal nearly always wins. We must have the ability to carry on in spite of temporary setbacks—to carry to completion a task undertaken. But is this strength entirely as we Americans have conceived it?

Ben Kadowaki, our Japanese gardener, loves to tell me about the culture of his homeland. Recently, he pointed out the symbols of strength in the garden. The Tao religion recognizes water as the symbol of strength. It conforms to everything that it touches, yet

Viewpoints of a Commodity Trader

has the power to force its way through rock. Another symbol of strength in Asiatic culture is the bamboo. It bends with the wind. When the wind passes, it regains its upright position. How many of us have the wrong concept of strength, the one that is so brittle that it breaks with the wind instead of yielding? The Japanese science of jujitsu is based on the principle of winning by yielding.

To me, strength is found in that which is durable. For this I nominate the spider's web. It's there after every storm while oaks have fallen.

A Time To Rest

THERE IS A TIME TO PLAN, a time to do, a time to stop, a time to rest!

Do you ever find yourself in the position where the things you are doing are pushing you, where you are afraid to stop trading for fear you will miss a grand opportunity? If so, there is danger you are near the "point of no return"—compulsive trading. We term it "tradeitis"—trading for the sake of trading. This often leads to trading fatigue.

I have known very successful traders who, afraid to take a vacation for fear something important would happen, eventually lost their "touch." One such individual is reported to have lost more that $4,000,000 over the past five years.

When faced with such a situation, it's time to ask yourself two fundamental questions. First, is this the only opportunity that will ever come my way? Second, if this is such a great opportunity, am I mentally, physically, and financially prepared to take full advantage of it?

If the answer to either is, No, it's time to stop and

Viewpoints of a Commodity Trader

rest. It's time to let the soul catch up with the body, to give yourself the chance to think a little clearer, to plan a little better.

I have done just that, or rather, I have made the attempt. While these attempts are not always successful, I believe this one was.

I have spent three weeks in Europe contacting people who are well informed on the fats and oils and the soybean situation throughout the world. I must admit some feeling of guilt about having missed the drop in July soybeans and the weakness in meal but feel confident that there will be many more such moves in the period ahead. As of now, I can say with assurance that I am ready for them when, and if, they do come. And what is important, I will be doing the pushing. I have had time to do a little relaxed thinking.

Distractions

AN ASSOCIATE suggested this subject. He is a successful, experienced trader. During his early struggle, he found himself beset by so many possibilities that he became distracted by them. He owes his success to specialization. His specialty is soybeans—*only on the long side.*

Some by nature are suited to the bullish side; some produce best as bears; others can do best as spread traders.

George G. and Dan C. came to visit us. They are successful brokers. One specializes in hedging and the other in spreading (for profits with tax advantages). Each in his own way has found the activity best suited to his skill. Each has developed his God-given gift as any other artist would do.

Down through time has come this truth:

> A bull sometimes makes money.
> A bear sometimes makes money.
> But a pig never does.

Viewpoints of a Commodity Trader

Balthasar Gracian, a Spanish Jesuit, wrote 300 years ago:

> "Prize intensity more than extent.
> "The best is always few and rare . . . extent alone never rises above mediocrity; it is the misfortune of universal geniuses that in attempting to be at home everywhere, are so nowhere. Intensity gives eminence, and rises to the heroic in matters sublime."

Man's nature has changed little over the centuries.

Concentration

MR. T— would like to become a great commodity trader, the kind of a trader who can take $1,000 and pyramid it into $1,000,000 and know that he can do it again. He has the tools in terms of desire and knowledge. But, like most of us, is slowly losing his powers of concentration by dividing time between too many things.

Too many traders assume that one can be a concert pianist and a museum painter simultaneously. Trading is an art; to be great requires the same concentrated effort as any other art. Concentration means the ability to control your attention and focus it on a given problem until you have solved it. It means complete self-mastery. The constant switching of attention can eventually destroy the power to concentrate on anything for more than short periods. This is not sufficient time to find the little things that are vital. "It's the thing you learn after you think you know it all that really counts."

Concentration in commodity trading means thinking; it means planning; it means time out to meditate, time out to investigate, to research, to analyze, to evaluate, and to select. Too many traders simultaneously result in being "A jack of all trades, but master of none."

If you feel there is merit in diversification, then know there is also danger. Too often all goes wrong simultaneously. This challenges one's stress point. Compulsive trading may become a habit. It often leads to carelessness. If there is an offsetting profit, one is tempted to fight the market in the loss trade. Wishful thinking is always a possibility.

The danger is the gradual deterioration in one's ability to concentrate. This usually occurs so gradually, but progressively, that one is not aware of it until too late.

It is your choice to choose between the frenetic ant-like activity of the average (and below) trader, or the serene, leisured but more productive heights of the above-average trader.

The art of concentration can help you to become a great trader. Knowledge of the art alone is insufficient. It must be practiced.

Fighting a Market

"Some men are as sure of what they think as others are of what they know."

Doc called this week to discuss a problem that all of us face at some time. He found himself fighting the market.

How many times has each of us, having set out on a course, thought it necessary to continue because we have begun? Somehow our pride or prestige becomes involved. We feel that it is important to seem to be right whether we are or not. There is great danger in this thinking, especially when we become so blindly convinced of being right that it is difficult for us to recognize that we are wrong and, more important, to admit that we are wrong.

When one fights the market, he tends to be run by the market. He no longer trades because he has a good reason. He trades because he must. Why? To save his pride. This then becomes living proof of the

Viewpoints of a Commodity Trader

scripture which says, "Pride goeth before a fall."

When one fights a market he is using energy and time that can and should be better used to do creative thinking. He becomes a compulsive trader. He no longer is the captain who is following a well thought-out plan. He trades because he must. He has become a victim of his folly.

When we are wrong and know it, there is no other way in which we can keep straight with ourselves except by admitting it.

Ride Your Horse

IN THE CAVALRY the sergeant's command was, "Ride your horse. Don't let your horse ride you."

Bill L. recently took a refresher course in commodity trading with us. While here he spent weekends at Ranch Roy-L riding horses. I noticed that he picked the slowest "nag" the first time out. When chided about always bringing up the rear, he commented that he had never yet been thrown from a horse. But it was also obvious that each time out he picked a horse with a little more spirit.

Bill is from the city. His experience in horseback riding helps me understand the advice given by Professor Theodore H. Brown of Harvard. When asked how to make money with money in commodity trading he answered, "Split your profits right down the middle and never risk more than 50% of them again in the market."

It takes time to learn to be a capitalist. It takes time to increase one's knowledge. It takes time to raise the tempo of one's disciplined courage. It takes time to train one's energies. It takes time to push further away the boundaries of one's stress point. It takes time to learn to ride a better horse.

Sometimes profits in commodity trading come in windfalls. When this occurs it is wise to follow Professor Brown's advice and Bill's practice: Pick a horse you can ride; limit your trading capital to what you can manage with your knowledge, your disciplined courage, your energies and your stress point.

I have found from experience that if one follows the advice of Professor Brown and the example of Bill, he will go a long way toward solving the age-old problem in speculation: "It is easy to make money—the difficulty is in keeping it."

It was Confucius who said: "When prosperity comes, do not use all of it."

Stress Point

I HAD NOT BEEN IN THIS BUSINESS very long before I came to realize that some traders were consistently able to do much more than others with a given market situation. As time passed, and my experiences increased, I came to know some traders who had lost everything and yet come back. Others folded and never recovered. Some traders seemed to have the knack of holding on successfully when others who had also been knocked down (in the very same arena) stayed there.

I found myself wondering why traders so very much alike in so very many respects often reacted so differently in the same market situation. Since the basic market situations involved were the same for the traders, I began to look for differences in the men themselves. Clearly, it was not always a matter of superior knowledge or greater skill. Quite often, it seemed to come down to a matter of confidence. And the degree of confidence with which each man traded seemed to hinge largely on the trader's adjustment to something which I came to think of as his "stress point."

Each of us, in our daily lives, tends to adjust to this invisible stress point. If a man lives just up to it, he can lead a happy and productive life. If, on occasion, he lives just a little over it, he finds that often these are the periods in which he learns by "running scared." If, on the other hand, a man lives too far over his stress point, that man will tend to panic. Sooner or later such a practice results in disaster. Finding the demands (financial or mental) too great, a man who follows such a practice, like a piece of metal bent once too often, will inevitably break.

But the real problem, for most of us, lies in setting our sights too low. Mainly because of fear, perhaps 95% of us live too far under our stress points. For those who dare too little, the penalty which must be paid, while perhaps not as sudden as for those who dare too much, is equally sure and certain. Life becomes dull and meaningless. Those who dare not become so much beef on the hoof; they exist, but they do not live.

No two traders should trade alike. What is right for one may not be right for another. Each should trade according to his own stress point. You are an individual. God did not make anyone else like you.

Viewpoints of a Commodity Trader

Why, then, should you think you will succeed by trying to imitate others in their methods of trading? The true formula lies in knowing yourself and in knowing your stress point. Then, and only then, can you be yourself at your very best. And that is the very best that you can ever hope to be.

Running Scared

"Running scared" is an expression we use to denote uncertainty in a particular trading situation. By definition, it means trading just a little in excess of one's stress point. Quite often I have used the expression, "I'm running scared—and enjoying it." I've come to realize that often it is during those times when I'm scared that I am happiest. While at first glance this may sound contradictory, it can be explained. True happiness does not come from doing an easy job. It comes with the afterglow of satisfaction which follows the achievement of a difficult job that demands our very best. Running scared permits one to behold the power of faith to work miracles as expressed in these inspiring words: "Fear knocked at the door, Faith opened it. And lo, there was no one there."

When one is scared (but not frightened, there's a big difference), he is stimulated to think. Quite often this is the only condition conducive to productive thought. Man is a lazy creature. We all tend to be as lazy as we dare to be. So long as affairs are running smoothly, there is a tendency to take things for

Viewpoints of a Commodity Trader

granted. We assume that the market is on course; that there is no need for concern; that there is no risk in this "best of all possible worlds."

But in the real world in which we live, change is the only thing certain.

And change has a habit of rudely awakening lethargic or complacent traders. Unless we sometimes find ourselves running scared, it is almost a certainty that we are not living up to our real potential. There are far worse things than occasionally running scared. The worst possible fate is to simply vegetate—to live so far under our stress point that we are never forced to think.

Running scared gives one a chance to flood the dark corners of fear and superstition with the bright light of reason and knowledge, overcoming fancy with fact, dispensing hobgoblins of the imagination and revealing the truth that is basic to our way of life.

The Chinese use the same symbol for danger and for opportunity. The truth of this seeming paradox has been brought forcefully home to me many times in trading. It is best illustrated by a statement from a successful young trader: "I knew we would not make any money on that trade. We never did run scared on it."

"Diamonds are polished by grit, men by adversity."

Mistakes

I HAVE ALWAYS BELIEVED that the greatest mistake in life is to give up. History is replete with successful men who have built their fortune on past mistakes. They were not afraid to make a mistake.

Our gratitude goes to an old friend and counsellor in speculation, Adolphe Reinstein of Rotterdam, Holland, for a concept about mistakes that is a shocker: "A trader seldom makes only one mistake. If he makes one, he usually makes two. It's the second one that hurts."

While I had never thought of it just this way, my experience and observation indicate that this is true. Human nature seems to respond to pressure in this manner. The harder we try, the poorer the results. It is only when we operate in a relaxed manner that we rise to our best.

Another observation on mistakes is that the trader who is right in his analysis 60% of the time and makes mistakes in less than 10% of his trades will make money. The trader who is right in his analysis 80% of the time and makes mistakes 20% of the time will lose money. We see this principle operate in baseball, football, and golf as well as trading. The real difference between winners and losers is not so much native ability as it is the discipline exercised in avoiding mistakes. What separates the amateur from the old pro is that the pro makes fewer mistakes. It is said that it takes two to five years to teach a college all-American to become a pro quarterback, who avoids mistakes.

Let's avoid making that first mistake. But if we do make it, let's avoid the second one. The first one may teach us. It's the second one that kills us.

Giving Up

A FAVORITE precept of President Calvin Coolidge reads:

> "Nothing in the world can take the place of persistence. Talent will not; nothing is more common than unsuccessful men with talent. Genius will not; unrewarded genius is almost a proverb. Education will not; the world is full of educated derelicts. Persistence and determination alone are omnipotent."

All around us we see those who have suffered misfortune. Some find a scapegoat to blame for all their troubles. This sometimes takes the form of "giving up" on a person who has been and can continue to be of great help. It even goes so far at times as to give up one's belief in God because we have not had our way.

In one of the cathedrals of England there is a beautiful window through which the sunlight streams.

Viewpoints of a Commodity Trader

This window was fabricated by a skilled artist out of broken bits of glass which another artist had discarded. This is a parable of life. Some people, because they have faith and persevere, are able to take the shattered bits of life and make them into something beautiful.

Let us be among those who learn from tragedies and turn adversity into opportunities and advantages to ourselves.

There are no impossible situations—only people who think so.

Hope(less) Trading

DR. B— made his annual visit last week. He had done very well early in the year. Then came the two successive mistakes. Now he is taking time out to bleed a little and to nurse his wounds.

It is a great mistake to take chances with one's stress point. This is what one does when he overtrades. Over-trading in its many forms leads in the end to reliance on hope rather than skill.

Reliance on hope is the greatest risk. This can become a bad habit. Once started, particularly if successful once or twice, it is difficult to control.

The greatest loss is loss of self-confidence. There are many traders who have lost all they had and have come back. One can do this more than once providing he never loses his will. Where there is a will there is a way.

What does a trader do when he nears the point

of loss of self-confidence? He must resort to the most powerful force in the world—positive thinking. He must believe he can. Remembering past successes helps. It is important that he prove that he "can" by selecting just one trade he can operate without error. This does not mean a trade without risk. It only means he can operate it without making a mistake.

If self-discipline is needed, command yourself to do it, and then force yourself to do what needs to be done. Such an experience is not without its compensations.

The most glorious moments of one's life come when, out of a period of correcting mistakes, one finds a new interest in life as a trader and a promise of future achievements.

Luck

THERE ARE COMMODITY TRADERS who believe that luck alone is responsible for their success or lack of it.

"Some get the breaks. Some don't."

When I hear this it gives me the creeps. I think that the person who believes it has "gambler's disease." When his luck is poor, he can't quit because his luck is bound to change. When he is succeeding, he can't quit because he is on a "hot streak."

I much prefer to think as Knute Rockne taught us at his football coaching school—"those who get the breaks earn them."

Certainly there is such a thing as luck—being in the right trade at the right time.

However, there is a great difference between reliance on luck and reliance on pluck. In the end, a commodity trader will stand or fall on his ability rather than on chance. There are traders who cannot profit from "good luck" when it occurs because they are not ready. They take small profits in big moves.

Viewpoints of a Commodity Trader

A successful commodity trader will follow Napoleon's admonition—always allow for a chance error as well as calculated error in action. In that way he can stay alive until the break he has earned adds to his success.

Forecasts

ONE OF THE GREAT MISTAKES made by some traders is to assume that all forecasts are perfect. Others make the equally great mistake of assuming that all forecasts are bad. Good trading practice uses the forecasts that are right but protects the trader when the forecast is wrong.

It is possible to make it big in trading if one has a clear idea of direction, degree, and timing. One must know when to buy, when to sell, and when to stay out of the market. Necessity requires our best efforts in forecasting. There is no lazy success in trading. If you assume perfection in a forecast, you are doing it the easy way. Impossible! You are going to have to work for it. If you are not able to adapt yourself, if you are not willing to get down in the mud and crawl occasionally, you may be a forecaster but you certainly are not a trader.

If we begin with certainties we shall end in doubts. But if we begin with doubts and are patient in them, we shall end in certainties.

The superior trader will never admit that it is possible to forecast perfectly. He does this out of necessity for self-preservation. If he permits himself to have certainties, his mind becomes dull. Dull minds are not capable of quick movement.

A good trader will never hold to his views too firmly. He knows that, "Every fool is fully convinced and everyone fully persuaded is a fool." Do not expect a perfect forecast. They are rare.

Over-confidence in your knowledge of the market may deprive you the grace necessary for success. One must have faith in his knowledge, but that faith is not adequate unless it is faith that permits doubt.

The analogy I like best when describing the art of trading is that of a contestant in fencing. One rule is constant: you cannot perform very well for very long with your shoes nailed to the floor. In trading, as in fencing, there are the quick and the dead.

Statistics

STATISTICS ARE MUCH ABUSED by some. Many who use them do not understand their value, and many who should use them ridicule them instead. They are very useful if used properly, but can be most harmful if improperly used.

What then is their value? They are somewhat like that part of the iceberg which can be seen. Seven-eighths is below the surface. Only one-eighth is visible but that one-eighth is very important. It shows the voyager where the remainder lies.

The experienced analyst knows that if used in conjunction with other tools, statistics can be most useful. The problem arises when in desperation we force ourselves to believe that they are the complete answer and that under any and all circumstances it is possible to find an answer by the statistical route.

When faced with these problems, I remember the advice given me as a youngster by the late John

Viewpoints of a Commodity Trader

Holmes, Chairman of Swift & Company, "If statistics can help us solve just one big problem a year it will more than pay its cost."

My experience is that statistics can do this very well. Be grateful if they do more but do not expect it.

Look Before You Leap

ONE OF THE GREAT MISTAKES made by commodity traders is impulsive trading. Too many, too often trade helter-skelter; one day short, the next day long; one day in soybeans, the next day in bellies. Continuous trading tends to become a disease. What has happened is self-hypnosis which leads one to believe he knows more than he really does. A little learning becomes dangerous. Because one knows something, he tends to believe he knows it all.

It is always well to "look before you leap." These steps will help. Ask and answer these questions:

> What do I know?
> How should I conduct myself to
> be in harmony with what I know?
> What are my beliefs?

Viewpoints of a Commodity Trader

The danger is that one will always find in his search for the truth that which he wishes to find.

The answers are not always easy to find. But one can always try by taking time out to reassess values, each in his own way. For myself, I have found the careful writing of an operating plan well ahead of action to be helpful.

If one will get the facts, analyze the facts, build a program of action, and follow the program, he will be well on his way to looking before he leaps again.

Tips

I ONCE THOUGHT that somewhere there is somebody who knows the answer to market direction and degree. After many years of searching and contacting the best minds, I now believe that there is nobody who knows and that nobody ever will know.

I have never been able to make as much money on someone else's ideas as I have on my own. Nor have I ever seen anybody else make and keep substantial sums of money on ideas not their own.

In spite of this experience, it is my belief that vast sums are lost each trading day on "tips." Many traders are waiting for tips, waiting to be told what to buy or sell. The explanation probably lies in the observation made by Mark Twain: "Only 10% of the people think. 10% think that they think. The other 80% would rather die than think."

Another reason for so much trading on tips can be attributed to necessity. Most brokers live off commissions. For the average brokerage house, tips become a form of chain advertising. A good flow of tips is considered good merchandising. Tip-seekers and tip-takers are invariably tip-passers. Tip-broadcasting becomes an endless chain.

Tip-takers are slaves to habit. They have difficulty resisting the craving and look forward to those tips indispensable to their happiness. To be told precisely what to do to be happy in a manner that one can obey is the next best thing to being happy. The belief in miracles (something for nothing) that all men cherish is born of immoderate indulgence in hope. Substituting hope for fact is the greatest risk. It is not speculation as practiced by successful traders. How much better to follow the advice of Huxley, "Give me the strength to face a fact even though it slays me."

Aside from the fact that tip-takers never get rich, there is another and more vital reason to resist all invitations to trade on tips. The great satisfactions in life never come from something without effort. There is nothing that will put you out of the running as a trader quicker than a soft snap. Minds need difficulties in their schedules, just as bodies need roughage in their diets.

Why take the hard way? Why not turn our hearts to the soft answers? Because the soft answers simply do not work. The only answer is the hard way built on the solid rock of reasoning and experience. This is a very dangerous, uncertain world. Nobody else can solve your problems.

Viewpoints of a Commodity Trader

Run from the tip as you would from the plague. Adopt the attitude that "I don't know it all; you don't know it all; and I am afraid of the man who thinks he does know it all."

Regard the tip-passer as one who knows not and knows not that he knows not.

Out of Control

HAVE YOU SEEN TEENAGERS weaving in and out of traffic as if they owned the road? How many of our traffic fatalities are due to adults acting like teenagers?

It is true in trading, too. I know of men today who are taking dangerous chances with their money and, more important, unwarranted risks with their self-confidence. They are running the risk of losing valuable assets which include poise, ability to think clearly, and ability to make good judgments. In several cases, men are becoming irrepressible addicts to the evils of speculation. They think that they must risk everything they have on each and every move. In other cases, brokers are finding uncertain trades to keep their clients' money working and, I am sure, to keep the commissions rolling in.

The most pitiful tragedy in this fascinating, profitable activity of commodity trading is the "might-have-been"—the powerful man who had everything but who refused to yield to controls. He did as he pleased. His capital and ability were dissipated.

Viewpoints of a Commodity Trader

The man who goes to the top as a commodity trader does not do as he pleases. He submits to controls, to discipline. He brings his desires into line by channeling his resources and strength into the trades that have a high potential and a high degree of certainty. He has trained himself to choose correctly between the two freedoms: the freedom to do as he pleases, and the freedom to do what he must do.

The stronger the man, the more necessary the controls.

Do You Lie To Yourself?

YOUR TRADING CAPITAL is your "seed." It is one of the two tools vital to success in commodity trading, the other being your ability to think.

It is important when considering your capital that you know at all times exactly what your capital position is.

One of the most important decisions you will make in commodity trading is how to manage your seed. It is vital that you recognize that you are engaged in a program that is of major importance to you. When you take this attitude you can start to build a program in keeping with your resources, your temperament, and your knowledge.

I have seen too many strong men, successful in other businesses, wake up in a panic when they have lost too much money for their temperament. They had planned to put up more when, and if, it ever happened. But when it did happen, they suddenly became aware of the fact that they could not take it.

Far too many traders, particularly the amateurs, hide their heads in the sand when adversity comes and hope that the paper losses will go away and somehow be replaced by paper profits. Or they suddenly decide that should they lose their seed they will add additional capital from some other source to the trading venture. It is very easy in time of adversity to assume the role of the hero and take it on the chin. All of these procedures are fatal to success.

That is no way to run a business. Successful commodity trading is a business. The most successful traders I know always take money out of the market. They never put any more money into the market.

The people who look upon their capital as something they can lose in commodity trading are taking the view that success is a matter of good luck that will some day run out. These people lose money. The successful traders live by rules that they know will guarantee success if they are followed.

For purposes of keeping daily score, it is recommended that you add each day the profits in open trades to and subtract the losses in open trades from the cash balance. In this way, you will not lie to yourself as to how much capital you have for trading purposes.

The biggest fool in commodity trading is the man who lies to himself.

Know the Score

IN TRADING, one must be constantly alert to protect his resources. This represents the defensive phase of trading. A good defense is basic to success. Here are a few simple calculations that are recommended for those who wish to build a good defense. It is urged that you keep score on each item daily.

Defensive information:

1. Available capital
2. Margins
3. Gross power
4. Net power
5. Calculated risk in open trades
6. Percent of capital risked.

Calculating the above items will give you the information necessary for survival. It will help you to keep from losing your capital. But knowing how to keep from losing your money is no guarantee of knowledge about making money.

To make profits, you must appraise the opportunities. Like a good farmer, you must seek out the most fertile soil and plant your "seed" when the weather is favorable. This is the offensive phase of trading.

Offensive information:

1. Potential profit
2. Potential loss
3. Margin required
4. Profit/loss ratio
5. Profit/margin ratio
6. Degree of certainty (type of trade)

The calculation of these twelve items daily will permit you to do the one thing that will make commodity trading both meaningful and profitable. It will make it possible for you to choose between the action that you want to take and that which you must take. This is freedom in the truest sense.

Keeping Score: Calculating Risk

IN THE ANCIENT PORT of Genoa, the mariners had a saying, "Know your limits, and where you are, if you want to get where you're going." But in those days, if you were daring enough to sail out of sight of land, knowing where you were was always a problem.

From Genoa, almost five centuries ago, sailed Columbus, expecting to find a new route to India, finding instead a New World. He had to navigate chiefly by "dead reckoning," a most uncertain method, considering the enemies he faced: time, distance, and the trackless, uncharted sea.

Not until 1731 did John Hadley, an Englishman, demonstrate an instrument for navigation destined to become the forerunner of the modern sextant. This device would enable daring sailors to plot their courses and to calculate their position, reducing their risks and making their lives less hazardous. In other pursuits, as in navigation, plotting your course and calculating your risk usually pay dividends.

My college teammates and I never considered the possibility of losing. Some of our most humiliating defeats came as the result of overconfidence. Later, training to be military officers, we were taught the value of neither overestimating one's own power nor underestimating that of the enemy.

These lessons from the past can be applied to the present in commodity trading where your power is capital, and others in the market are your enemies. Just as the mariner relied on his sextant, I strongly recommend that each and every trading day you calculate your risk in open trades. Follow this practice faithfully, and you will always have a good idea of just where you are in relation to where you want to go.

Never risk all of your capital in one trade. Diversification is a good rule. Professionals, who can risk more on any one trade than amateurs, seldom do. Since there is always the possibility of surprise in thin, dead markets, less capital should be risked there than in markets which are broad and moving.

Many find it a good rule to limit the risk in any

one trade to a maximum of 10% and the risk in all open trades to a maximum of 25% of trading capital. Unless the market presents an unusual opportunity, some traders keep risk in any one trade to 5% or less and in all trades to 15% or less of trading capital. Risk should always be calculated as a percentage of available capital (equity). Determine this each day, adding profits and subtracting losses in open trades, and combining this net figure with your trading capital.

The above may seem somewhat academic, but it is just as important as one's appraisal of the market. I've seen far too many traders get careless about calculating their risk, about knowing their own particular score, about knowing where they were in relation to where they were going. This mistake is usually fatal.

Be a good trader: do your homework each day.

Keeping Score on Selectivity

Do you play bridge? If so, do you bid "seven spades" on every hand or worse yet, "one spade?"

It has been rightly said that life is a matter of selectivity. There are opportunities each day. The question is, "Which ones do I select?"

How does one go about the important job of selecting the best trades available to him? Trading is still an art. There is no substitute for good judgment. But there are some measurements that can assist one in his decision.

I have found that the ratio of "profit expected" to "potential loss" is a quick reminder. I am more impressed if the potential profit exceeds the expected profit.

Since it is very unlikely that you will make a profit on every trade, it is important that you develop skill in the art of selecting those trades which will make

Viewpoints of a Commodity Trader

you more money when you are right than you lose when you are wrong. The trick, of course, lies in accurately appraising the profit that can reasonably be expected as well as appraising the loss potential.

This is an area in which an experienced researcher (or trader) has an advantage over the amateur. There must be no wishful thinking in such an appraisal. The ratio of "profit expected" to "margin required" is of passing interest only, since one should always have available capital in excess of margin requirements. However, should the margin requirement be substantially less in one instance than in another (as is usually the case in straddles), I give it weight.

Whether you do your selecting with the help of the tools described above or by some other means, it must be done.

Do You Allow for Error?

MARGIN IS THE MINIMUM CAPITAL required by a broker to finance a trade. This figure is usually set by the clearing association. It is but a small fraction of the price of a commodity. July corn may be $1.15 per bushel. The broker may ask only 5¢ per bushel as margin. This means additional capital will be required should the trade move adversely.

Many traders, particularly the uninformed, make the mistake of depositing only the minimum margin required. For many, this results in disaster. Either it sets in motion the habit of putting up more and more capital as the price moves adversely or, equally bad, it results in a hasty decision based on fear. Fear must be overcome and bad habits must not be permitted to develop.

I find it best, when calculating the capital requirements for a trade, to allow for errors—errors in judgment plus chance errors. This policy has proved itself many times. When the war erupted in September, 1939, I was short in the market. Had I not allowed for the possibility of war, I would have been closed out at a disastrous loss. The market went up the limit on three successive days. Actually my power permitted me to sell more at the top of the market. I came out of it with a nice profit on the drop in October.

For purposes of keeping daily score, regard the margin required as being constant. Changes in price result in changes in equity. These changes should be added to or subtracted from your capital.

It is important to always keep in mind that your margin is committed. It cannot be used to finance any additional trades. How much of your capital you will have on deposit with your broker is an individual problem. Pros can get by on less than beginners. I strongly recommend that you always start with more than the minimum required for margin.

The most successful traders allow for chance error as well as calculated error when financing a trade.

Power

WHENEVER MARIS OR MANTLE appears at bat, we are reminded that they have power. Other players have power too, but less so. We all have power to some degree. The problem is to know how much we have at any moment and how best to use it.

When I left the farm to attend high school in the city, I had plenty of vim, vigor and vitality. I could run rings around the city boys in athletics. I made the teams easily, but my city pals did much better than I later in the season. One of the most valuable lessons in life was taught me in a close game when the coach let me sit on the bench while he pointed out to me the ability of our top scorer. This chap was not wearing himself out by always running at top speed. He always seemed to have the ability to do just a little bit better when the chips were down. He waited for his chance and then gave everything he had.

When keeping score in commodity trading, one must always know what he can do next. This means knowing your gross and net power. Gross power is calculated by taking one's capital and subtracting the margin required to carry open trades. For example, if one has $2,000 capital, and has an open trade of 5,000 bushels of corn which requires $400 margin, then the gross power is $1,600.

Net power is calculated by subtracting from gross power the capital that may be required to carry open trades through possible adversity. For example, should your gross power be $1,600, and should you anticipate the possibility of carrying one contract of corn through 6¢ adversity, then your net power is $1,300. This amount represents the only money that you have to enter another trade. The balance of the $2,000 capital is committed.

Like a general in a war, there are two great mistakes that a trader can make. First, he can lose all of his capital. Second, he can fail to take advantage of an opportunity. If all of his capital is committed, he does not have the net power to fully exploit unexpected changes.

The most successful traders are always in a position to take aggressive action.

Net Power

MOST TRADERS ARE AWARE of the funds deposited in their trading account. Some are aware of the daily changes in equity. A few, too few, know the gross power in their account at the start of each day.

Hardly anyone takes the time to calculate net power daily. I have long regarded it as one of the most important tools in successful trading in commodities. I am sure I do not know enough about it. The important thing is to correctly calculate net power daily.

Why run the risk of sacrificing freedom by failing to calculate net power properly? Leave yourself a choice. It is a sorry state when net power gets to a position where it is impossible to make even one change in plans.

Perhaps the most serious problems that arise from a lack of knowledge of net power lie in the area of the mind. I have long regarded loss of self-confidence as the greatest loss to a trader. One can lose money and recover it. Once self-confidence is gone, throw in the towel. If one meets with frustration after frustra-

Viewpoints of a Commodity Trader

tion because of lack of net power to carry through on plans and aspirations, he eventually gives up.

Commodity trading can be fun or it can be a nightmare. The concept and use of net power can make the difference.

Too Much Capital

IT TAKES CAPITAL TO TRADE. Some traders do not have enough while others have too much. Capital is power. So, too, is knowledge and understanding. The ideal situation is when there is a proper balance between the two.

When there is too little, one often tries to do too much with too little and ends up frustrated. When there is too much capital, one is tempted to use it improperly.

An illustration is the case of the college boys from Princeton during the Henry Kate episode in wheat during 1959. They believed and expressed the thought that "money is power." The evidence does indicate that they did contribute to the rise in wheat prices during February and March. Their knowledge of wheat did not permit them to get out at the top.

Another illustration is the wheat market of 1898

when Joe Lieter tried to carry his corner into June. It collapsed.

If one must err in the balance between knowledge and capital, it is probably safer to err on the side of too little capital. Then you can know what St. Paul meant when he said, "When I am weak I am strong." One often does what one must do. If capital is low it is necessary to acquire knowledge and understanding.

In reality, it does not take much capital if one has knowledge and understanding. There have been, and will again be, markets where one can multiply his capital a hundredfold within a year.

The Moment of Truth

THE "MOMENT OF TRUTH" is that magic moment when the facts are known that firmly set the course of the market. Most of the time, one must take a position on inadequate and sometimes faulty information. Usually, the market has discounted the important facts before they become known at least when known to most of the amateur traders. For example, one may take a short position in September eggs today in anticipation of a surplus of eggs this fall. The "magic moment" will not occur until we know that the chick hatch has been increased—until we know that these chicks have become pullets and are laying eggs. By that time, the market will probably be lower than it is today.

Quite often the market anticipates something that never happens. You, too, will often do so if you trade in commodities. We witnessed such an event in corn.

Viewpoints of a Commodity Trader

Many traders bought corn in the fall in anticipation of large loan entries. This may still happen. But the dominant force has been, and may continue to be, the large scale selling of corn by the Government.

It is important to remember that the magic moment is when the important facts are known to those who can influence market action rather than the moment when you know them. One must always be alert to get the facts first.

It does not follow that the market has always discounted the facts at the moment of truth. There have been instances when the market had made such a serious mistake that much time was required to correct it after the dominant facts were known. Such a case was the Henry Cate attempted squeeze in May wheat in 1959. The market was so much on fire that even after it was known that wheat was moving into Chicago in volume, a trader could take a position with assurance of a good move downward. Such instances will occur again.

Be alert to detect that rare "moment of truth" when you can put your mind at ease about the situation.

Silence

SOME TRADERS TALK TOO MUCH. They talk too much for their own good. There are very good reasons why one should keep what he knows to himself; one reason is enough.

Every time you tell somebody what you know, you sell yourself on its importance. It is possible to hypnotize yourself into believing something simply by repeating it enough times to other people.

Talking too much tends to become a problem for many solicitors because of the nature of their work.

Speech may be silver, but "silence is golden." Traders with the golden touch do not talk.

The Touch

IF YOU HAD YOUR CHOICE between $1,000,000 and "the touch," which would it be? For many, probably for most, it would be the million. For me, it would be "the touch." With it comes the ability to make that million and more in addition to having fun doing it.

What is this "touch"? Call it what you will—a knack, a feel for what you're doing, an awareness. We sense its presence in many different activities, as well as in commodity trading. The benefits are usually easy to see. Many of us have a friend with a "green thumb" for growing things. Another friend will take blue ribbons at the fair most every year.

In trading, too, some men have the touch. I know men who have it now. I know men who had it once and lost it. It is not difficult for a man who has it to pyramid a few thousand dollars into millions. I have seen this happen. It is all too easy for a man who does not have it to lose all he has. I have seen this happen, too.

So this touch is valuable. But what is it, really? To define it precisely would be difficult, and perhaps im-

VIEWPOINTS OF A COMMODITY TRADER

possible. But I think I know what a man has when he has it. He has an extra portion of awareness, of sensitivity, of comprehension of the world around him. He has foresight, as well as knowledge of past markets. He sees a developing storm and measures its effects before others even know it's on the way. He's the main stream of life. He's part of the passing parade, but he's usually a few steps out in front, and he's marching to the sound of a different drummer.

Can the touch be acquired? With hard work, with the right attitude toward yourself and the world around you, yes, I think it can. Can it be lost? From long and careful observation, I know it can. Trading without good reason, chancing (replacing facts with hope), trading continuously and even to the point of fatigue, overtrading without due regard for capital or individual temperament—these are only some of the common errors that cause good men to lose their touch.

If you have neither the touch nor the time or inclination to develop it, hire someone who has it to make money for you. Find him and pay him well. It will be one of your very best investments.

Professionals

DID YOU WATCH the Packers whip Kansas City in the Super Bowl? I did and was much impressed by the professional way in which they performed. They did not beat themselves by making mistakes.

A professional makes fewer mistakes than others. That is why he is a professional. He may not have more ability than another but he is superior because he has trained himself not to make mistakes.

I was particularly impressed in watching the Packers throughout the season as they seldom were penalized for infraction of the rules.

This lesson has direct application for us as commodity traders. It's not too late to resolve to be a professional. Let's not beat ourselves by making mistakes. We can become professionals by knowing what mistakes are, by training oneself to act in a manner to avoid them, and by exercising discipline (will power) to carry out the training.

Do you want to be a professional? Will you pay the price?

Commodity Trading, a Service

COMMODITY TRADING is engaged in by most to make money. It is speculation, not investment. There is no way to put a bum trade in your safe deposit box, as many do stocks until the price rises.

As speculators in commodities, we willingly and knowingly assume risks for the purposes of making a profit. As such, we perform a service long accepted and recognized by legislators and the courts.

In the words of Justice Oliver Wendell Holmes:

> "Speculation . . . is the self-adjustment of society to the probable. Its value is well known as a means of avoiding or mitigating catastrophes, equalizing prices and providing for periods of want.

Viewpoints of a Commodity Trader

"It is true that the success of the strong induces imitation by the weak, and that incompetent persons bring themselves to ruin by undertaking to speculate in their turn.

"But legislators and courts generally have recognized that the natural evolutions of a complex society are to be touched only with a very cautious hand . . ."

We can and should find pleasure in being of service to our fellow man.

Declining Commodity Markets

Declining markets mean rising profits for an increasing number of successful traders who know that profits can be made on the short side of the commodity markets. This message is written to extol the merits of bear markets.

My observation and experience lead me to the conclusion that it is possible to make as much profit on the short side of markets as on the long side, and probably with greater assurance. Declining markets are usually of the realizing kind and less often make big mistakes by going far below their true economic value.

After a market has made a mistake on the upside, it is not too difficult to recognize the mistake and to know how far down it must go to correct that mistake.

Viewpoints of a Commodity Trader

It takes fuel to keep the bullish fires burning. But a market will fall of its own weight in the absence of bullish news.

A bear has good company. Industry hedging is much more stable and certain than are the long positions of speculators.

Perhaps one of the more important reasons for trading a declining market is that sequence trades are possible. The opportunity to recoup is much more likely to occur if a trader loses on the short side. Market rallies that are false can be reinstated after a mark time stop. If the market rally is the beginning of a long rise, one can reverse his position when the evidence seems more certain that a sustained rise is in the cards.

I like the short side of the market because there is less company. The mob is usually wrong. It is usually long.

It is as easy to sell as it is to buy. One is performing the same service on the short side as on the long side. In either case he is helping society by tempering the shock of abrupt change through accepting the risk as a speculator.

The uninformed commodity trader would do well to learn how to trade declining markets. It is a step in the direction of becoming a successful pro.

Overtrading

THE WORD THIS TIME is overtrading. I must confess that I have had much trouble with this phase of trading. What does it mean? It is all bad?

In nearly every book on the subject of speculation, you will find the admonition, "Do not overtrade." This is one of the few laws absolute that frustrates me. I am sure that it means different things to different traders. To one, it means an over-extension of market position because of limited capital. To another who has the capital, it may mean over-extension of nerves. Many times it means paralysis of action because of inability to think clearly. Evidence is strong that it is present when one must reduce one's position to be able to maintain another, or when one replaces fact with hope.

We must agree that overtrading is bad, by definition. Anything done in excess of one's capacity must be so classified. The difficulty arises when one tries to apply the rule. Each one should trade differently. Overtrading for one is not overtrading for another. One can lose all his capital and come back again. It has happened all too often. Some learn what they can do, only by a process of trial and error. The danger to avoid is loss of self-confidence.

Let me remind you there are two things a successful speculator in commodities must have—capital and sleep. In practice, I strongly urge that you so act as to keep the mind clear and the judgment good. If you find it hard to sleep, reduce your position some or all.

A good general never risks all of his troops in the front lines at one time. He is always ready to take advantage of a breakthrough when it occurs. Be a good general.

Spread Trading

MANY COMMODITY TRADERS are not aware of the profit possibilities in spread trading. I know some who run from it as from the plague. There are those who love it. Most of those who understand and practice spread trading do very well at it. My information leads me to believe that most of the successful, experienced professionals practice spread trading.

First, let me describe a great danger in what amounts to a malpractice in this art. Some traders believe that they are spread trading when, in fact, they are practicing deception. These traders start by establishing a net long or net short position. When it goes against them, they attempt to cover their mistake by taking an opposite position in another contract month in the same commodity or in another commodity. Sometimes these traders start with a spread and later lift one side to establish a net position. Successful as such practices may be for some, they often lead to confusion and losses for most.

The advantage to spread trading applies solely to those trades that are started and closed as spreads.

Viewpoints of a Commodity Trader

There are many advantages. First, the change in spreads is often more predictable than is the direction of a market. Second, capital required as margin is usually less than for net positions. Also, the change is usually gradual since it is influenced less by surprises such as war scares, crop scares, and government announcements. Another advantage is that spreads work on advancing and declining markets.

The best reason for taking an interest in spread trading is that probably a larger percentage of those practicing it make money than do those who take net positions. It's not foolproof, but it does have some advantages.

Trading the Fundamentals

CHART TRADING is interesting and will keep you alive in a world where few traders survive. But the objective in trading is to make profits and to make them big when there is opportunity to do so. Trading the fundamentals, armed with a thorough knowledge of what they are, is the key to the big profits.

Most traders who depend upon their own knowledge and interpretations of fundamentals do less well than those who trade on charts. Too many pure fundamentalists are under-schooled and ill-equipped. Like most men, they think they know more than they really do. They have difficulty in separating fact from rumor.

Human nature works against the fundamentalist. We all like to be right. It is difficult to admit error.

A secret to successful trading is: "Cut your losses, let your profits run." He who trades on fundamentals too often hangs on when he is wrong and takes big

Viewpoints of a Commodity Trader

losses. The commodity market is no place for heroes. A fatal mistake made by the fundamental trader is to take small profits. This, I feel, is the result of limited vision—extremes always seem silly to men of so-called good judgment.

Successful trading on fundamentals is difficult but not impossible. Few men have climbed Mount Everest but it has been done. If one will pay the price, one can accomplish the near impossible. The price, in this case, is to spend one's time on learning more and more about less and less instead of dissipating one's energies by learning less and less about more and more. In other words, the answer lies in specialization. This is a full-time job. You are working toward precarious heights where "a little learning is a dangerous thing." Knowing something is not enough. It's the thing you learn after you think you know it all that is important. You must know it before it is discounted in the market, and you must not know something that is not so.

For most traders, the answer lies in seeking help from someone who specializes. The wisest men are those who know and know that they know.

Chart Trading

WE HAD A SUCCESSFUL WRESTLING TEAM at the University. Charley Mayser taught us well the use of a few simple holds. Our competitors often knew many more tricks, but we won. When I think of chart trading, I am reminded time and again of the principle, "shoemaker stick to your last."

There is much valuable information that a trader can observe about the current situation in any market by keeping a complete set of charts. Such information includes the following:

> Is the market active?
> Is a significant formation or pattern developing?
> Is liquidation or accumulation occurring?
> Is the trade or the public dominant in the market?

This is only a partial list of the important information a trader can obtain daily by observing chart action of price changes, changes in open interest and

Viewpoints of a Commodity Trader

volume of trading, and changes in spreads between options and between commodities.

There are some real advantages to the use of charts in trading. These include timing entry and exit; limiting losses; maintaining your position in the big move; keeping part-time traders appraised of general price trends.

There are also some real disadvantages to the use of charts as the only tool in trading. Those who depend upon charts have difficulty appraising value. Most are downright poor analysts. Many do not think it possible to analyze the market correctly. Some are content with success based on chart approach and will not make the surpreme effort required to accurately appraise value.

It is not possible to carry large positions on the basis of chart actions alone. There is a limit to what the market will take on any day. Quite often, the market is temporarily thrown off course by those who trade on chart action only.

Those who trade solely on chart action should be prepared to take many losses and a few profits. If properly managed, this can be profitable, but it is psychologically difficult.

Charts Plus Fundamentals

I AM OFTEN ASKED, "Are you a fundamentalist or a chartist?" It is as if East is East and West is West. For most traders this is true. It need not be. There is merit in merging the two.

Life in the country is rough at times. Because it is real, the lessons learned are not soon forgotten. One truth, observed on a dark night in the rough terrain surrounding our "Twin Echoes" country house, has helped me to understand the necessity for merging charts and fundamentals. Our family, including the children, were on a hill across the creek from the lodge. Each step of the way was rough going. At some points it would be necessary to reverse our direction to avoid trees and large boulders. In the darkness we could see the lights in the lodge, our ultimate destination. To find our way past trees and boulders and across the running water, we

Viewpoints of a Commodity Trader

used flashlights. Now I understand the function of fundamentals. They are like the beacon light in the lodge. I also understand the function of chart action. It is like the flashlights we needed that dark night to avoid bumping into trees and boulders and to keep from falling into the creek.

The market is a very tough, complicated, competitive business. Easy money is hard to come by in commodity trading. A fair degree of success calls for a fair degree of study and hard work and understanding of the market.

Thoroughness and quality count for more than speed in the long run. The fable of the hare and the tortoise reminds us that the race is not always to the swift. Chart trading is apt to develop a tempo too fast for one's temperament. We need to pace ourselves in our trading activity. Trading only when you have a good reason based on an appraisal of fundamentals and using chart action for confirmation and timing of entry and exit will help to give satisfaction to your feeling of accomplishment and contribute significantly to your economic welfare.

Your Broker

SOME COMMODITY TRADERS get nothing but headaches and big losses. Others have fun and make profits. The difference might be your broker. He can be an important part of a successful team effort. He should be expected to place your orders properly and report executions promptly. He can also be expected to be aware of pertinent facts. Well-trained brokers can help some traders solve their problems in such matters as trade selection and money management. A few outstanding brokers have the skill to match the temperament of a trader with types of markets. Some brokers can do their job better than others.

Everywhere we look we find mediocrity. This goes for lawyers, carpenters, doctors, dentists. The list has no end. Why expect all brokers to be outstanding? They are not. Only a few are, as in any other profession.

Even if he is tops, it is unrealistic to assume that every broker will click with every trader. A broker is a human being with irritabilities and problems. If he is a capable broker and well trained, he will recognize the customers with whom he cannot establish a good relationship and will turn them over to another broker.

If you are having difficulty making a profit with your present broker, it might be a good idea to consider a change. I have known of traders who did poorly with their first two brokers and the third one produced the miracle. The change in brokers need not be to another brokerage house. Very often it can and should be from one broker to another in the same firm.

The Big One!

THE BIBLE relates a parable told by Jesus that has application:

> "Behold a sower went forth to sow; . . . . some seeds fell upon stony places, where they had not much earth . . . and some fell among thorns . . . . But others fell into good ground, and brought forth fruit, some a hundredfold, some sixtyfold, some thirtyfold."

Some traders, who enjoyed the soybean market of 1960-61, have asked, "When will it happen again?" This is the one type of market that permits an experienced trader to parlay $10,000 into $1,700,000 within six months. Another parlayed $15,000 into $150,000 in three months. Still another made $280,000 from $60,000 in thirty days. This happened within the past 12 months. When will we have a market that will permit building such fortunes again?

This is a most important question to most traders

even though they trade the small moves too. It is the one big move that makes it possible for a trader to take 9 losses and one profit and come out in the black.

This is possible in commodity trading where one cuts his losses short but lets his profits run. As with the British, who have the reputation of losing every battle but the last one, it is not necessary to make a profit in every trade.

I know of traders who became discouraged with the mediocre results of 1958, '59 and '60 and picked up their chips and quit. Those who persevered through 1960-61 realized that what had not happened in the previous three years could and did happen in sixty short days in 1960-61. The net results for the period were amazing.

The move such as occurred in 1960-61 in soybeans does not occur every year. Since 1950, there have been five such moves in soybeans. There was a gap of four years between 1955-56 and 1960-61.

While such moves occur rarely in a specific commodity there is usually a move of moderate degree in some commodity each year. In 1956-57 it was oil; in 1957-58 it was cocoa; in 1958-59 it was meal; in 1959-60 it was meal. The Big One may or may not occur this year. It's worth waiting for.

Playing the Big One

A MOST IMPORTANT QUESTION that each trader must answer for himself is, "Why trade anything but the Big One?"

I have known some who only play it for the big money. My previous boss, Mr. A. F. Seay, had the patience, knowledge, wisdom, and character to do so successfully. Far too often, those who play it this way do not have adequate information to pick the Big One. It is difficult to forecast them. Or, they make a negligible amount compared to what can be made. Or, they may lose their heads completely. I have known people who have been carried away by quick large profits that were beyond their expectations.

The answer to this question must be different for each trader. For myself, I find the profits and knowledge gained from trading in the smaller moves most helpful in taking full advantage of the Big One. "The heritage of the past is the seed that brings forth the harvest of the future."

Another question of great importance when the Big One does occur is, "What should I do about it?" There are many traders who did not make money in last year's Big One. They did not know what to do with the ball when they got it. To take full advantage of such a move, one must be prepared mentally for it. Believe that it is possible. You must be there when the Big One gets going. Second, have the power to act. Third, be rested mentally and physically. The Big One is exhausting. Fourth, play it right. Let your profits run, cut your losses quickly. This is a different program than one uses on the little moves. You can pyramid the Big Ones.

Winning the Big One is not unlike winning the World Series in baseball or the National Open in golf. It does require some experience and ability. Making big money on the Big One is not easy, but it is possible!

The Easy Way

THERE IS IN OUR WORLD TODAY the idea that one with money can make more money quickly. Commodity trading is one of the ways. It is not too difficult to make money in commodity trading. The problem is to keep it. There are people who do.

Far too many commodity traders have been sold the illusion that somewhere somebody knows what the market is going to do. They little realize that much more is required than the best knowledge of the market. Self-reliance, good judgment, courage, prudence, pliability, perseverance, humility—these are stepping stones in the trail that leads to profits.

Most of us have seen in our time phenomenal developments in the production of goods and services. Automation leads one to believe that we can make short cuts in all that we do. The difficulty arises when we attempt to apply this principle to the building of people. One cannot grow in ability faster than he lives. It still takes time to gain experience. We can't find self-reliance where it does not exist or good judgment when it hasn't been planted and devel-

Viewpoints of a Commodity Trader

oped. We can't pour courage, prudence, pliability, perseverance, and humility as we do concrete. There is only one way to do it, the hard way. We may revolutionize a business in three proven steps, but look twice at anyone who wants to teach a trader how to make a fortune in three easy lessons with a minimum of effort.

Those who believe that they have found a short cut to success are very often on a rough detour. Those who believe they can ignore the rules and disregard proven practices of successful commodity trading are not even gambling. They are playing a sure game—the result is 100% certain. They will lose.

Many years ago we had four plays in pro football: through the line, around end, a pass, and punt. Most of the time we punted. We scored rarely. Today pro football is much more complicated and successful. Each player must learn many plays. Each player is thoroughly trained to do his job perfectly. There are few punts and many scores. The team that wins is the team that makes the fewest mistakes.

The easy way is nearly always the hard way. It is often the only way. No other way ends up where we want to go.

Dreams

IN ONE OF THE ST. LOUIS OFFICES there hangs a sign, "You don't have to dream to work here, but it helps." I would like to add these few words: "Dream Big Dreams."

It has been my observation that few people set goals too high. They are content to use but a fraction of their ability.

Next year could be the Big One. The stage is set for another experience where a few thousand can return millions. But one thing is sure; it will never happen if you are content with a 2¢ profit in a bull soybean market.

Why does "Dreaming Big" work? I am not sure. The important thing is that it does work. There are so many examples of success where one has practiced the concepts contained in these thoughts:

> "What the mind can conceive and believe it will achieve."
> "Thinking heroically makes heroes."
> "As a man thinketh in his heart, so is he."

Viewpoints of a Commodity Trader

"A man becomes what he thinks about all day long."

Of course, there is a great difference between wishing and thinking when one is Dreaming Big Dreams. Nature will not be cheated or deceived. There is no such thing as something for nothing. Only continuous, unyielding, overwhelming, persistent effort will carry us to our goal of high achievement.

Dream Big Dreams and Think Tall. I dare you to accept this challenge. It will pay.

A Trip to Purdue

WE JOURNEYED TO PURDUE for the purpose of leading a discussion on commodity trading. The trip was truly eventful, but the discussion was more so. I have been stimulated to answer the question put by one professor, "Do people trade for purposes other than to make money?"

The answer, of course, is Yes. There are those who are compulsive traders. There are others who find commodity trading a challenge.

Commodity trading is a unique way of life. It can be slave or master.

Commodity trading is a two-edged sword. It will provide the means to accomplish your dreams or it will cut you to ribbons.

Commodity trading is a stage, and the role you play in the drama of life is up to you.

Viewpoints of a Commodity Trader

Commodity trading is a way of thinking through which you can reach higher than you ever have before.

Commodity trading is your right to be yourself, to fail and try again. Commodity trading always gives you another chance.

Commodity trading looks beyond the problems of today to the promised land of tomorrow.

Commodity trading has its head above the clouds, but its feet are bedded in the solid rock of disciplined thought and action.

Commodity trading takes big risks; it dares the moon flight.

Commodity trading lives with hopes for the future. It may never realize them, but it keeps reaching.

Mistakes are bound to be made, but try to avoid making the same one twice.

Commodity trading is the art of using money to make money.

Commodity trading is the art of paying the price for something you want.

It is the art of regarding fear as the greatest sin, and giving up as the greatest mistake. It is the art of accepting failure as a step toward victory.

It is the art of seeking with the knowledge that

you will find; knocking and knowing that doors will be opened unto you.

Commodity trading is the art of being yourself. There are as many ways of trading as there are people.

It is the art of being bold when courage is required. It is the art of using good judgment for which there is no substitute. It is the art of being prudent when caution is required.

It is the art of being pliable; bending with the wind is often the price of survival. It is the art of persevering in the face of adversity. It is the art of humility. It is always possible to learn from others.

It is the art of recognizing the liar as the most dangerous person in the world, particularly the man who lies to himself.

It is the art of sticking to fact knowing that the greatest folly is substituting hope for fact. Commodity trading is the art of being a clever man. The one who does what he thinks is right.

It is the art of using the most potent force in the world—positive thinking. It is the art of taking advantage of the greatest opportunity—the next one. It is the art of gaining the greatest victory—victory over self.

It is the art of overcoming the greatest handicap—

Viewpoints of a Commodity Trader

egotism; the most expensive indulgence—hate; and the most ridiculous trait—false pride.

It is the art of knowing that the greatest loss is not money but loss of self-confidence; and that the greatest need is common sense.

The Hall of Mirrors

OUR JOURNEY in the field of commodity trading takes most of us eventually to the Hall of Mirrors, so called because in it we can see only ourselves. Many traders are there today. They see only success. They think that they had something to do with the profits they have made. Little do they realize that they may have been right for the wrong reasons.

Very few will realize in time the danger that exists—that there is constant change, that their wish is now father to their thoughts, that facts are being ignored and being replaced by hope and that arch enemy, greed. Little do they realize that most of the people who have made money in these markets will lose it during the next 100 days.

This trip has been taken by most of the large traders as well as the smaller ones. It is not an exclusive affair. Joe Leiter took it in the famous bull market

Viewpoints of a Commodity Trader

in wheat in 1898. He had enormous profits in early May of that year. He lost it all and more too when he decided to run his corner into June.

What do we do about it? One of the greatest traders of my knowledge gave me his secret in these words: 'When I am long with a large profit, I get my car and leave town. At each town I come to, I call back to the office and reduce my position." This man is still going strong in his 70's.

Mr. William H. Danforth, founder of Ralston Purina Company, expressed it to me in these words: "Have you taken a loss? Forget it quick. If you have taken a profit, forget it quicker."

Baron von Rothschild is reputed to have answered the question, "To what do you attribute your success?" with the words, "I always took my profits too soon."

When you find yourself in the Hall of Mirrors, where the air is close and the company boring, break the mirror. Make a window and breathe fresh air. Get a new perspective so that you are free to think and act.

Advice

SOME TRADERS DIE from too little advice.

Many think that to seek advice indicates weakness. The contrary is true. To seek advice means that one is well advised.

In commodity trading, it is impossible for anyone to know it all. A matter of great importance is to know those who know best. The man who thinks he does is seldom the one.

Others die from too much advice. There are those who seek the advice of all, even the barber. How foolish they are is indicated by the fact that there are services which succeed by contrary opinion. When a high percentage of advisory services are either bullish or bearish, the probabilities are in the opposite direction. Too much company should always be feared by the trader. When everyone is bullish, there are no new buyers.

Boxed In

DURING WORLD WAR II, I was much impressed by a statement attributed to General Marshall, "I cannot afford the luxury of getting mad at anybody."

In commodity trading, we must make the decision—do we want to succeed. We can do so if we are willing to pay the price.

The price very often means accepting the services of others who are not perfect.

I recently witnessed a serious flaw in analytical work by an otherwise capable individual because he closed his mind to help offered by one against whom he held a prejudice.

We should look for help wherever we can find it; from friend or foe. All that matters is, "can it help me do a better job in trading commodities?"

Results are better in our trading if we learn not to expect too much from others. We can strive for perfection in ourselves. To expect it in others is madness.

When disappointed in others, we can forgive and forget.

Viewpoints of a Commodity Trader

It is a measure of excellence to absorb anything that is positive.

Let that which is negative hit the veneer of a thick skin and disappear as if it doesn't exist.

All are boxed in by what they know.

Each has the power to make the box larger and larger.

It is possible to learn something from everybody.

Good Information

THE GREAT IMPROVEMENT in communications should be a boon to commodity trading. It can be a handicap.

I heard a story recently that illustrates the problem.

Three lines of varying length were visible to 25 men thus:

```
#1   _____
#2   _____
#3   _____
```

Twenty-four of the men were instructed to say that #1 line was the longest. When it came to the last man (uninstructed) to give his opinion, he reluctantly agreed that perhaps #1 was the longest.

We are all familiar with what happens to information when it is passed from one person to another. It never comes out the same.

Good information seldom comes by way of the ear. It is nearly always biased by positions in the market or by unwillingness to disagree with the majority.

That is why rumors for a time can dominate a market. All that is needed is a good story that inflates the imagination. If the move is reasonably limitless, so much the better.

Good information needs to be seen. One should question the source of any information that comes by way of the ear.

Thinking and Learning

SOME PEOPLE KNOW that learning is important. Most traders know that a little learning is dangerous.

It sometimes happens that those with much learning find themselves at a disadvantage. The Go Go markets, that rise for no good reason, catch the seasoned, well-informed trader off balance. With more and more new people coming into the commodity markets, we can expect markets to become more exotic. When this happens, it seems that thought without learning succeeds.

If you know anything about past markets, you seem to be too old to participate. The market seems to pay attention to the wildest of rumors. This can, and does, go on for a time; sometimes for a long time.

Always in the end, there arrives unheralded the Black Knight of Panic. His invincible flashing saber quickly cuts down, without mercy, those who linger

Viewpoints of a Commodity Trader

too long, and proves once again that—thought without learning is very dangerous.

There is, of course, the other side of the coin. Some would-be analysts have great learning and that is all they have. They know so much about the past that they live in it. To be productive as a trader, one must be in tune with the past, present, and future. This is a changing world. Cause and effect relationships do not remain constant. History never repeats exactly. Just as no two persons are ever exactly alike, no two markets move similarly in minute detail.

Those who depend on learning alone sooner or later prove that learning without thinking is time wasted.

Realizing Bull Markets

REALIZING MARKETS can be either bear markets or bull markets. There have been more realizing declining markets than realizing advances.

When one is faced with a realizing bull market, he has an unusual opportunity. The direction is highly probable and the degree of rise is often large. Sometimes the rise occurs in a relatively short period of time. The risk is usually small.

The characteristics of such a trade are:

1. A fundamentally bullish situation.
2. A reluctance by the speculator to buy.
3. An inversion or small carrying charge between cash and futures.
4. Business interests may be either cautious or bullish.

VIEWPOINTS OF A COMMODITY TRADER

These conditions are rare. Some illustrations are:

The meal market of 1965-66.
The corn market during the summer of 1923.
The belly market during May-July in 1965.

Risk Control

IF THERE IS ONE SECRET to success in commodity trading, this is it.

Most traders who ignore risk control know not what they risk.

They think that all they risk is money. Actually much more is at stake; life itself. I am not discussing here vegetable existence—but life.

The commodity trader who has life, has above everything else—will; the will to do. This can be, has been, and will be many times in the future, killed by an absence of capital; particularly after one has had it. A commodity trader would do well not to ignore this psychological fact in his program.

Life is everything to a trader. When one has it, he can wear his tie the way he likes; he can set his own goals. He can be absorbed in his purpose, and give expression to his passion for acquisition and possession.

For a trader with life, desires are not timid aspirations but unavoidable impulses. For their sake, he will accept the dangers of a market position. His

Viewpoints of a Commodity Trader

courage exceeds his virtue. When a trader has life, he has powerful ambitions. He despises limits. He bows to nobody nor does he emulate another. He likes a tumultuous life. Peace to him is for old age. It does not become a man.

There is no return from extinction. When a trader's will is gone, he is dead.

Knowledge is not enough. It never is. Courage is also needed.

Risk control is not denial of freedom. On the contrary, it is the only thing that does permit freedom to act. Without capital, courage to act is diminished as is the power to act. Freedom is the existence of choices. No capital—no choice.

It does take courage to live. The brave die. What a price to pay to prove that one is brave.

Processed Data

NEARLY ALL COME TO DEPEND on information that comes through somebody else. Before it gets to us, it has been modified in some way. Sometimes it is colored by bias. Even unbiased government figures are subject to error because of faulty sampling.

The amateur cannot do much to overcome the inherent faults of data that he uses. Professionals can and should smell out the weaknesses in the figures they use.

Not all situations can be adequately described by words and figures. We are concerned about how people feel and think, and how they react to a situation.

Sometimes the only way one can get a feel is to take the overnight bag in hand and go to find out for oneself as a general visits the front, or as a general salesmanager calls on customers.

Much of the time, processed data is reliable. Sometimes it becomes necessary to get the vital facts through a feel of the situation by first hand contacts.

The Story

WHEN WE WERE CHILDREN, most of us were put to bed by a fairy story. As we grew older, most people realized those stories for what they were.

Unfortunately many people who trade still respond to the fairy stories. The only requirement is that people believe it to be possible.

A trader cannot ignore the stories that are at variance with reality. For the time being, the only thing that is important is how long will people believe it. If the story is contrary to fact there will, of course, be a day of reckoning.

Weather Markets

A SMALL GROUP of "oil scholars" met at the Ranch over the weekend. An outstanding contribution was made by Armand Iaccheo of the Weather Corporation of America.

In essence he told us that:

> Forecasts of weather beyond a few days are not reliable.
>
> Temperature forecasts are more reliable than are forecasts of moisture.
>
> Sometimes it is more difficult to forecast moisture for the next six hours than to forecast temperature and rain for the next three days.
>
> There are times when a forecast of rain is more reliable than at other times.
>
> Sometimes the degree of certainty approaches

Viewpoints of a Commodity Trader

100%. But it never reaches 100% until after it has happened.

The fact that someone has been able to forecast weather accurately once does not mean that he can do it every time.

Given the same conditions he can probably duplicate his performance. But, the conditions are seldom the same.

All that the above facts mean to yours truly is that weather markets are:

Mercurial.
Extreme in price fluctuations.
Very difficult for the trader to master.

I am intrigued with the possibility of quick, substantial profit opportunities on those rare occasions when a qualified weather forecaster can predict rain with a high degree of certainty—particularly when the market is vulnerable.

Pliability

I HAVE FOUND that rigidity is one sure way to lose time and money in commodity trading. One must learn to be pliable, to adjust quickly. Commodity trading is a constant exercise in adjusting to whatever happens. Nothing ever seems to develop exactly as expected in price changes. We are dealing with the reactions of man—not with a science.

Whatever happens in commodity trading, as in life, one must keep on going. There is a certain amount of disappointment that all must take, and there is no use getting upset about it.

There comes a time when you have to face hard facts and be able to take things as they come. The successful trader develops the ability to take what comes, meets it calmly, keeps his mental processes operating, and does the best he can.

St. Paul learned to be content in whatever state he found himself. He drew on the deep sources of philosophical understanding—as every trader must do if he wants to adjust quickly to price moves as they occur.

Viewpoints of a Commodity Trader

In our business, we are always looking for the greatest opportunity. One cannot do anything about yesterday. When one door closes, another door opens. The greater opportunity nearly always lies through the open door.

Trade Selection

SHOULD ALL TRADERS be encouraged to buy wheat if the evidence indicates a rising market?

Most brokers mistakenly think yes.

The truth is: Some should; some should not.

In commodity trading "one man's meat is another man's poison."

To get the right answer as to who should be encouraged to buy, one should ask the right questions, such as:

> How much risk is involved?
> Is the trade a part of a campaign—or is it just one trade?
> What effect will a loss have on the will of the trader and on his power to trade?
> Is there a better trade now or later for this trader?
> Is the trader able to watch this trade closely?
> Is the trader, by nature, pliable or rigid in his trading habits?

Viewpoints of a Commodity Trader

These and other factors make much difference in the answer to the question, "Who should be encouraged to participate in each trade that becomes available?"

The ultimate in trade selection is to match the character of the trade with the character of the trader.

Classification of trades and classification of traders helps to do this.

The Deepest Secret

A GREAT CHANGE for the better occurs when we learn the secret taught by Jesus as He prayed—"Not My will but Thy will be done."

The market has a will. In the end, its will prevails.

It is not given to any man to know it all. When he thinks that he is the smartest man in the world, he puts himself in a class we call fools. They should be shunned in the market. These teachings in the Christian religion have great meaning to us as traders: "Seek and ye shall find, knock and it shall be opened unto you."

Those who discover this deep secret suddenly come alive. Everything they do now takes on new meaning.

Why?

Because they are no longer being shown. They are discovering great truths for themselves. They have found a way to bring newness into their lives.

Viewpoints of a Commodity Trader

There are those who sit and wait for the world to change for them. Some few guess correctly that they are the ones that must change. In commodity trading one usually gains by yielding, by admitting that he needs help, that perhaps there is a better way.

Have you, too, been hardheaded about clinging to the one way to trade a market? Can you think back to other instances when your tested procedures failed and how you found the answer just as soon as you changed your idea about how it should be done? Do you remember how when you accepted this fact that there was then a store of experiences and knowledge that rushed in to help you find the solution?

But, it only happened after you admitted that there was possibly a different way to do the job.

Will Power

THE DEEPEST SECRET for the trader is his ability to subordinate his will to the will of the market.

The market is truth in that it reflects accurately all the forces that bear upon it.

As long as he recognizes this, he is safe. When he ignores it, he is lost.

Pressure

Who is there today who is not under pressure? We have come to believe from experience that the wheel that squeaks gets the grease.

It is very dangerous to assume that this is the way to get desirable results in commodity trading.

I have seen it happen too often to be ignored. Pressure does bring results. It brings answers, but more often than not it brings the wrong answers.

Does an artist paint a masterpiece because he must or does he do it to give expression to something within him?

Commodity trading is an art. So, too, is good price appraisal which is so very vital to good trading.

Many, too many, customers ignore this truth. They believe that if they bring pressure on the broker, he can in some way do a better job for them. This same mistake is often made by brokers and management in their attempt to get more and better price appraisals from statisticians.

People, by nature, want to please. In analysis this quite often leads to wishful thinking when under pressure. Hope replaces facts. Facts can be selected to support a theory.

What we need in commodity trading is the right answer. Better few in number and right than many and wrong.

Fool's Disease

MANY WHO ENGAGE in commodity trading are killed by too much action and too little knowledge. There are those who die of too much knowledge and too little action.

A trader should be on guard against this illness, particularly after a series of losses. The tendency then is to wait on the next trade until he is sure—100% sure—that it will be profitable. Such a state of certainty is, of course, impossible. It is serious when one comes to believe it is so. He tends to become totally convinced. In such a state of mind, one ignores good trading practice. In the end, this is his Achilles' heel. And then weakness develops when one waits for 100% knowledge before acting. Very probably some part of the price move has already occurred. The risk is greater if analysis is wrong. The stop point is farther from entry. This limits the potential profit and increases the risk.

Statisticians, to their detriment, are subject to fool's disease. They never seem to get enough data to justify a conclusion. There is a very good reason for

Viewpoints of a Commodity Trader

their reluctance to commit their thoughts. To them, it is more important not to be wrong once than to be right 100 times. Their reputation is like the sun. It takes only one cloud to blot it out.

One should not expect to be right every time he trades or makes an appraisal. It is better never to let yourself believe that you are 100% sure of anything. Only then can you feel safe in commodity trading.

Plan to be wrong sometimes. The results will be more profitable.

Research

"Is Mr. Researcher always right in his market position?"

"No."

"Well then, I have as good a chance of being right as he."

This conversation has occurred many times in thought and speech. It will occur many times in the future.

Does everybody have the same chance of success in commodity trading? Who is most likely to be right? Is it blind chance?

I have long believed in research. Research is not always right. It does not have all the answers today. But research can help. Each bit added to other bits of knowledge improves our chance to reach excellence.

In some ways our activities are like baseball. The hitter who averages 300+ is more valuable than one who bats 200. Yet on any one occasion either may hit a home run.

A researcher does not know it all. But he probably has the higher batting average.

Viewpoints of a Commodity Trader

The manager usually plays the 300+ hitter. Research is now available to all commodity traders who will use it. All can be 500+ traders. That is optimum in this league. It is better for the pocketbook if we do not expect perfection.

Bad Research

THERE IS GOOD RESEARCH.

There is bad research.

The bad research drives out the good research.

To be of any value in trading, research must be very good or it is bad.

The reason: In this business it's the thing that you think you know that is not so that hurts. Good research is not easy to come by.

First of all there are very few trained statisticians who are qualified to do research. I have never seen one short of five years of training. In our business, the luster of the quick dollar usually attracts the most capable researcher to some phase of trading.

Secondly, one cannot do good research unless he devotes his entire time to it. Much of the so-called research in the area of commodity prices is done part time under pressure by biased minds.

Good research meets with great resistance and very little satisfaction. Human nature always takes the position:

Viewpoints of a Commodity Trader

I am right—when things go well.
You are wrong—when things go wrong.

These words from the Sermon on the Mount have great meaning to a trader who depends on research:

"Beware of false prophets. . . ."
"By their fruits you shall know them. . . ."
"A good tree cannot bear bad fruit,
  nor can a bad tree bear good fruit."

Unfortunately that is the only way most traders identify good research. Some few look before they leap.

Courage

To trade successfully, one needs two things:

> Knowledge
> Courage

The knowledge you can learn or buy.

Courage cannot be learned or bought. You either have it or you don't. But you can't succeed without it.

Money is the name of the game of commodity trading. When the opportunity for large profits is present, you must strike while the iron is hot. At such times you must make many times as much as you lose on each of your loss trades. If you make a little money on the big moves that occur only rarely, you might as well quit. You are likely to experience a series of loss trades. So you must make it big when the opportunity presents itself.

Courage is of two kinds in commodity trading. One kind is when you back your knowledge when things are going your way. The other kind is when

Viewpoints of a Commodity Trader

you have the courage to quit when things are going against you.

The great danger is in confusing courage with bravery. The market is no place for heroics. That is for another battlefield. In the market place it often takes more courage to live than it does to die. The greatest courage is the one that lets you graciously admit that you are wrong when you no longer have a good reason to trade.

The courage associated with the hero—(I can take it)—often destroys the courage that is needed to be successful. I have witnessed cases where temporarily successful traders have lost their touch because they lost their courage. They exceeded their stress point too many times. They became uncertain of their judgments. They sell when they should buy. They reduce when they should add.

It is a wise trader who knows his stress point.

Change

IN COMMODITY TRADING it is the only thing certain.

Somewhere a change is occurring that can make you rich.

Most of us are normal in that we expect the change to occur outside ourselves. A few are aware that the greatest change can be in ourselves. One of the great discoveries of our age is that man can change himself—that each of us becomes what he thinks about.

A number of years ago an executive, in the meat packing industry, remarked, "The thing that's wrong with the railroads is that they think and act like railroad men." It was my pleasure to have another executive in the meat packing industry call on me recently and hear him say, "The thing that's wrong with the meat packing industry is that we have not adjusted to change. We think and act too much like meat packing men."

One need only to look about him to see the simple truth:

Viewpoints of a Commodity Trader

That it is easier to change oneself than to change the market.

If we will pay the price by adjusting to the market we can have what we want.

Our greatest success will be the greatest victory—victory over self.

We can hope to profit by changes in the outer world. (We can be more certain by change in the inner world.)

All can face the future unafraid.

Exotic Markets

ALL MARKET ACTION is man made.

Markets in which speculative interests are dominant seem to be more mercurial in price movements. My experience leads me to place the following in the classification of exotic markets:

>Potatoes
>Copper
>Cocoa
>Bellies
>Cattle
>Eggs

There are probably others too.

These exotic markets, of course, offer opportunity for profit just as the more stable ones do.

However, it does require a different technique to do so. One who is successful in wheat, corn, and soy-

Viewpoints of a Commodity Trader

beans may not be in potatoes, bellies, and eggs, and vice versa.

It would be misleading to say that some commodities are always exotic in nature.

Given the right conditions any market may become exotic. Weather markets tend to be so.

What's Next?

IN THIS WORLD nobody is spared sorrow, tragedy, and the grief associated with his mistakes. The question is what to do about them. My former boss, the founder of Ralston Purina Company, always had one answer, "What's next?"

Nothing can mess up a man's life and increase complications like mistakes. It can be a steady and persistent drain on his energy, rob him of his efficiency, clog his mental and spiritual machinery, and cut down his drive to zero.

What does a man do with his mistakes, the failures, the defeats of the past? Like a hideous infection they pollute all his ambitions, dreams, and determinations for the future. Memory of mistakes drains his vitality leaving him weak and whipped.

True greatness comes this way. Until a man comes to the end of himself—until he reaches his extremity, becomes aware of his limitations—until he weeps over his own mistakes—he may be cocky, but never great.

Men like Edison, Pasteur, and Henry Ford survived hundreds of mistakes, failures, contempt, and loneliness, to win unheard of victories.

Faith teaches:

It's always too soon to quit.
Despair is never justified.
Because despair of self is really
to despair of God.

We can learn from mistakes, but only if we persevere.

A Prayer

Lord,
slow me down.
Ease the pounding
of my heart by quieting
my mind. Help me to know the
magical restoring power of sleep.
Let me look upward into the oak branches
and know that it grew solid, strong and enduring because it grew slowly. Give me strength,
courage, wisdom, vision, and a clear mind that I may
carry to fulfillment the responsibilities placed upon me.
Renew my energies that I may utilize to the fullest the talents bestowed upon me. When life has struck me a low blow, help
me to remember that this too shall pass. In times of prosperity,
remind me that the present is all that I have. Permit me to enjoy
it and find fulfillment. Permit me to persist in my pursuit of those
inexorable laws which if too long ignored will crush me but which
if observed can be the ever willing tool to accomplish Thy will.
Help me to understand that the real secret of happiness is to
learn to live within my limits
In good times
let me befriend
others knowing
that I will need
their solace in
my time of adversity. May I
ever be mindful
that not my will
but Thy will be done.

TRADERS PRESS®
INCORPORATED
PO BOX 6206
Greenville, SC 29606

*Books and Gifts
for Investors and Traders*

Publishers of:

Commodity Spreads: A Historical Chart Perspective (Dobson)
The Trading Rule That Can Make You Rich* (Dobson)
Profitable Grain Trading (Ainsworth)
A Complete Guide to Trading Profits (Paris)
Traders Guide to Technical Analysis (Hardy)
The Professional Commodity Trader (Kroll)
Jesse Livermore: Speculator King (Sarnoff)
Understanding Fibonacci Numbers (Dobson)
Winning Market Systems (Appel)
How to Trade in Stocks (Livermore)
Commodity Spreads (Smith)
Day Trading with Short Term Price Patterns (Crabel)
Understanding Bollinger Bands (Dobson)
Chart Reading for Professional Traders (Jenkins)
Geometry of Stock Market Profits (Jenkins)

Please contact Traders Press to receive our current catalog describing these and many other books and gifts of interest to investors and traders.

*800-927-8222 Fax 864-298-0221 864-298-0222 Tradersprs@aol.com
http://Traderspress.com*

•TECHNICAL ANALYSIS•OPTIONS•TRADING PSYCHOLOGY & DISCIPLINE
•SPREAD TRADING•ELLIOTT WAVE•W. D. GANN •INTRADAY TRADING
•TRADING STRATEGIES•

FREE TRADERS CATALOG

•FIBONACCI•FLOOR TRADING•FREE BOOKS (WITH ADDITIONAL PURCHASE)•MONEY MANAGEMENT•MUTUAL FUNDS•SHORT SELLING/ BEAR MARKETS•STOCK INDEX TRADING•SYSTEMS & METHODS
•MANY OTHER TOPICS•

TRADERS PRESS, INC. publishes a 72-page catalog which lists and describes hundreds of books, tapes, courses and gifts of interest to stock, options, and futures traders.
(Regular price $5)

Get a FREE copy by contacting
TRADERS PRESS, INC.®

TRADERS PRESS, INC.®
PO BOX 6206
GREENVILLE, SC 29606

Serving traders since 1975

800-927-8222
864-298-0222
Fax 864-298-0221
Tradersprs@aol.com
http://traderspress.com